Pushchair on Dartmoor

Emma Richardson

Bossiney Books · Exeter

First published 2022 by
Bossiney Books Ltd, 68 Thorndale Courts, Whitycombe Way,
Exeter, EX4 2NY,
www.bossineybooks.com

ISBN 978-1-906474-95-9

Acknowledgements
The maps are by Graham Hallowell
Photographs by Bronwyn Richardson

Printed in Great Britain by R Booth Ltd, Penryn, Cornwall

All the walks in this book were checked prior to publication, at
which time the instructions were correct. However, changes can
occur in the countryside over which neither the author nor
the publisher has any control. Please let us know
if you encounter any serious problems.

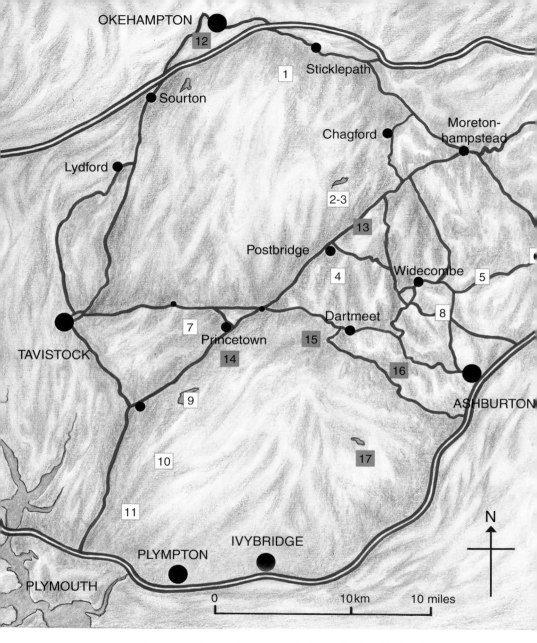

The approximate locations of the walks in this book.
Those in green squares are there-and-back walks.

Introduction

Walking with a pushchair

The walks in this book are designed to be suitable for all members of the family, but have been chosen primarily for their suitability for walking with a pushchair. The routes include interesting and varied parts of the moor and vary in length and accessibility.

All walks in this book have been tried and tested with an all-terrain pushchair; some are also suitable for any pushchair – including a stroller. The character of the terrain and paths are highlighted at the top of each walk description.

As with any outdoor activity, the walks are undertaken at your own risk and, particularly where babies and small children are concerned, you should assess the suitability of the walk for your own circumstances as you go.

When walking on the moor with a pushchair take your time, particularly over rough terrain and if your pushchair has a wrist strap do use it especially on hilly sections. Your child should also be strapped in using the pushchair's harness to avoid accidents.

Maps

The maps in this book are sketch maps and should be used for general guidance only. Anyone walking on the moor should carry an Ordnance Survey map of the area – OL28. (Walk 11 is on OL 20.)

Safety

The weather on Dartmoor can change very quickly so wear suitable clothing and footwear and be prepared for any eventuality. I recommend that you always carry waterproofs, water bottle, compass and map. In my experience of walking with children and babies, it is also a good idea to have some snacks with you too. Don't rely on mobile phone coverage to get you out of trouble as there is often no signal on the moor. I advise that you let somebody know where you are walking before you leave home.

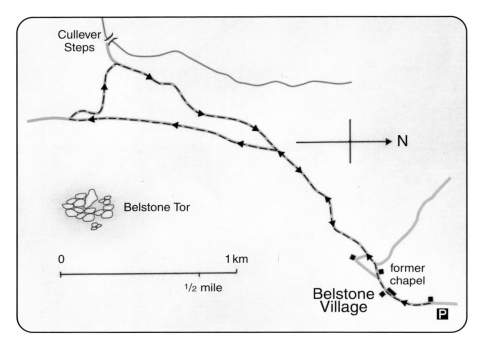

Walk 1   Belstone and Cullever Steps

Distance: 6 km   Pushchair type: All-terrain
Character: Starting in the beautiful village of Belstone, this walk
emerges onto the northern moor on distinct but bumpy tracks. A great
walk for taking in the expanse of Dartmoor, it is hilly in places and best
tackled with an all-terrain or sturdy pushchair.

Park in the Brenamoor Common car park (SX 621938) at the entrance
to Belstone. Turn left out of the car park and follow the main road
through the village. At the small village green where the road forks,
take the right hand fork walking past a former chapel, later the post
office.

Continue to follow the road straight ahead (no through road sign)
which climbs towards the moor. Go through the gate onto the moor
and continue to follow the track, initially uphill.

After 500 m take the track that splits to the left and follow it as it
contours around the base of Belstone Tor. The track is rough in places
and you may need to deviate to the left or right for short stretches.

After approximately 1.5 km take the distinct track that turns back
on itself and works its way down to Cullever Steps where several

tracks converge. Cullever Steps is the furthest point of the walk. Cross the bridges for an opportunity to stop and enjoy the view back up towards Belstone Tor.

Cross back over the two bridges and take the left hand track (NO MOD VEHICLES BEYOND THIS POINT). Follow this track back up the hill to retrace your steps through Belstone village and back to your car.

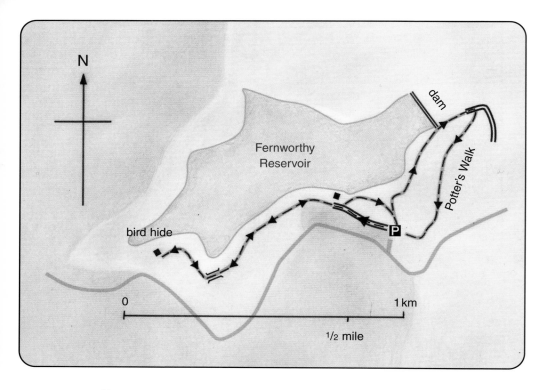

Walk 2 Fernworthy Reservoir: Potter's Walk

Distance: 1.1 km   Pushchair type: Any

Character: One of two suggested strolls along the banks of Fernworthy Reservoir, this one is really short and fully accessible. It passes Bronze Age hut circles and is the home of much wildlife. This circular route known as Potter's Walk was named in memory of Sydney Potter who lived and worked here for over 50 years. The well-surfaced track is easy to follow and passes several benches to stop and admire the view. Beginning and ending in the main Fernworthy car park, the route benefits from toilets and a beautiful picnic area to make the most of your day.

Park in the main Fernworthy Reservoir car park (SX 669839, pay and display) where the toilet block is located.

Leave the car park by the path at the bottom corner, keeping the picnic area on your left. Follow this track down towards the reservoir. As you near the bottom of this area the track bends round to the right, away from the picnic area.

Continue to follow this path over a small stream. The reservoir is now very close to you on your left. Fernworthy is home to a good stock of trout which can often be seen close to the banks. Heron, grebe and snipe come here to fish and there are often geese on the water – plenty of wildlife to look for as you walk along.

Continue to follow the path along the water's edge and you will shortly see the remains of a Bronze Age hut circle on your right. Dating from around 2000 BC, this was one of many in the area; in times of low water other circles can be seen emerging from the reservoir. As you approach the end of the path by the dam, there is a bench and an information board.

Pass this board and pick up the tarmac road straight ahead which crosses the end of the dam. Follow the road up the slight rise and take a sharp right onto the footpath just past the wheelchair assistance sign. Follow the track past the picnic benches and through the gate ahead into the wooded area. You will soon see a fence on your left enclosing one of the old quarries that provided granite for the dam. Continue to follow this path until you emerge back in the car park.

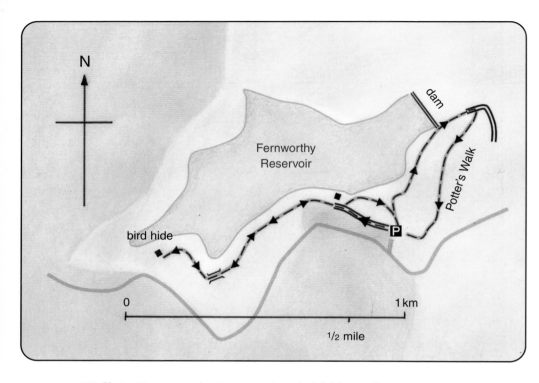

N

Fernworthy
Reservoir

dam

Potter's Walk

bird hide

P

0   1 km

1/2 mile

Walk 3   Fernworthy Reservoir: Bird hide walk

Distance: 2.5 km   Pushchair type: All-terrain/ sturdy
Character: A slightly longer walk exploring part of Fernworthy
Reservoir, which passes through wooded areas and ends at a beauti-
ful spot, perfect for a picnic or a sit on the shore. The walk also visits
a bird hide, the ideal position to spot swallows and perhaps a siskin or
woodpecker. Due to the rougher surface of the track and a couple of
uphill sections on the return route, this walk is suitable for all-terrain
or sturdy pushchairs but not strollers.

Park in the main Fernworthy Reservoir car park (SX 669839, pay and
display) where a toilet block is located.

   Leave the car park by the path on the right hand side of the toilet
block and follow the posts to the left of the picnic area turning right
onto the road. Continue along this dirt track passing the track to the
anglers' permission hut that you will see by the water. After approximately 150 m take the track up the slope marked ROUND RESERVOIR
passing through a gate.

8

This track rises and meanders along the hillside passing through a wooded area until it reaches a small bridge. Cross the bridge and you will emerge into an open area. Here, the path changes to a grassy track which bends away to the right. Follow this grassy track. The path goes up a small slope and then turns to the left. As you follow it round to the left, you will spot the bird hide – worth a visit to observe the swallows and other birds that frequent this peaceful spot. This is the furthest point of the walk.

To return to your car, retrace your steps until you reach the main track and the anglers' permission hut. Here, take the small track that emerges from the parking area just after the track to the hut. This runs diagonally down toward the water's edge and skirts the bottom of the picnic area below the car park. To return to your car take any one of the tracks up through the picnic area – the toilet block and car park will be visible.

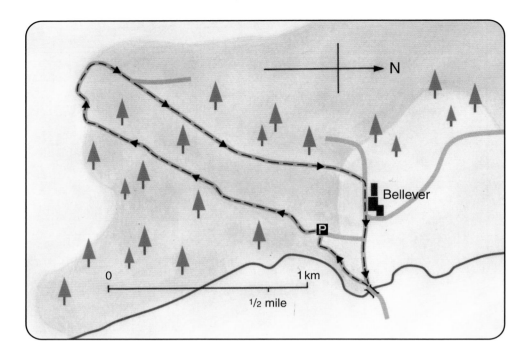

Walk 4   Bellever Forest

Distance: 4.2 km   Pushchair type: All-terrain
Character: A walk through Bellever Forest on mostly good tracks – one rough section towards the end requires an all-terrain or sturdy push-chair. The forest was planted in 1931 and contains a wealth of history, with many hut circles hiding in the undergrowth. You may also catch a glimpse of the Dartmoor ponies – a heritage breed that graze Bellever – or indeed a buzzard looking for his lunch. The walk ends at a lovely spot by the East Dart River not far from the car park.

Park in the Forestry England car park (SX 651771, pay and display); note the toilet block and information boards.

Leave the car park from the bottom corner – having passed the toilet block on your right. Turn right to walk through the area dotted with picnic tables, following the red post markers. Pass through the gate onto the wide gravel track straight ahead which starts to climb uphill. Follow this track for just over 1 km as it winds its way through the forest, eventually coming to a bend with a view out onto the moorland.

Follow the track as it bends to the right and around a further two bends. You will see occasional red post markers which indicate you are following the correct route. After a further 600 m the path forks. Take the right-hand fork which follows a downhill route, watching out for the camber on the track. Continue straight on for another 1 km at which point the track becomes a rougher path. The path emerges from the woodland between two fields: follow it until it reaches the road next to a farm.

Turn right onto the road and continue straight ahead; you are now walking through the village of Bellever. At the road junction just after the Youth Hostel, take the right-hand fork. You will shortly pass the entrance to the car park, but continue past this entrance to the bridge over the East Dart River. Just before the bridge, turn right, passing the old clapper bridge, and pick your way along the bank, watching out for occasional tree roots and uneven stones. After 300 m you will see a firmly surfaced track going off to the right. Follow this track back to the car park.

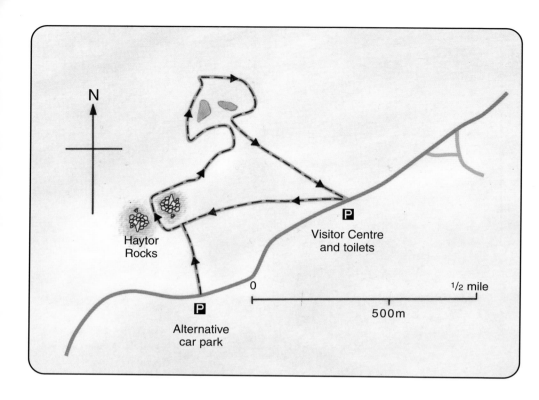

Walk 5 Hay Tor & Quarry

Distance: 2.6 km   Pushchair type: All-terrain
Character: The iconic Hay Tor is the backdrop to this short but steep walk. Due to the grassy tracks underfoot, this is only possible with an all-terrain pushchair. There is an option to complete the walk from an alternative car park as this popular spot can get very busy.

Park in the first of the Hay Tor car parks (SX 766771 pay and display) next to the visitor centre and toilet block. In the event that this car park is full, there is another further up the hill on the left hand side. See alternative route.

Cross the road and follow the broad green track up to Hay Tor rocks. This is a long hard push but worth it for the views at the top. As you approach the base of the Tor, veer to the left to skirt around behind the Tor, walking between the two outcrops. On emerging from between the outcrops keep the main stack on your right coming back around to the easternmost point of the Tor.

12

Take the track that heads downhill, walking towards the spoil heaps of Hay Tor Quarry in the distance. The track becomes more distinct and you will reach the fenced off quarry. Keeping the fence on your left continue downhill past the spoil heaps to the junction with a large track to find the gate into the quarry itself. Go through this gate. Beware of steep drops on the right of the path. This quarry still contains relics of the industrial site that it used to be.

Walk around the ponds to the gate on the far side of the site. Pass through this gate and a short distance further on at a path junction take the path that heads right, past the spoil heaps on your right.

Follow this path, turning right twice at path junctions. The third junction is with the track of the old tramway: turn right here, again following the track back around to the front of the quarry. After 150 m take the broad green track to the left which drops you straight back to the car park.

Alternative route. Park on the brow of the hill (SX 760767). Cross the road and take any of the broad grassy tracks up to Hay Tor. Once at the top, follow the route as above all the way to the lower car park. From the lower car park, walk parallel with the road back up the slope to return to your car.

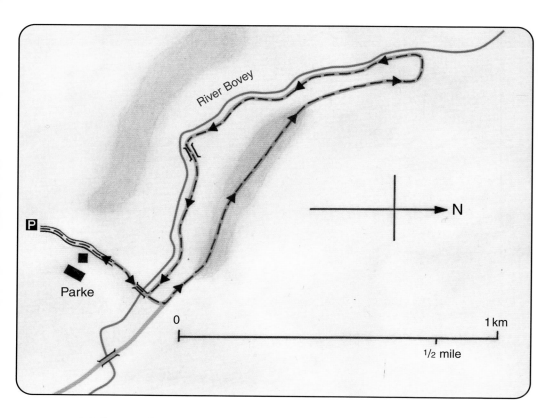

Walk 6 Parke Estate

Distance: 3.5km   Pushchair type: Any

Character: This circular walk is on dirt and cinder tracks with some muddy sections in wet weather. The tracks are mostly level with a couple of bumpy sections over tree roots towards the end of the walk. It is easiest with a sturdy pushchair but not impossible with a stroller. The walk takes you along the route of the former GWR branch line to Moretonhampstead and back along the river past a medieval weir.

Parking for this walk is in the National Trust car park (SX 805785, free for members or pay and display), well signposted from the main road.

Leave the car park from the bottom left-hand corner, following the metalled road downhill. You will see an orchard with picnic tables to the left, shortly after which you will pass a walled-garden and walk through the courtyard housing the National Trust café. Continue to follow the road past the buildings and down the hill.

14

The parkland to the front of Parke House opens out on the right hand side. Follow the path between fields and over two bridges – the second of these spanning the River Bovey.

Continue straight ahead across the open area as tracks branch off to the left and right. At the far side of the clearing, the track you are going to follow bends to the left and goes briefly uphill to join the route of the old railway. Turn left here and continue along this level track for just over a kilometre until you reach a left turn, just before a bridge that crosses the track.

This next section can be muddy in wet weather. Follow the path to the left downhill and then bear left as it starts to follow the line of the riverbank. Follow the river's edge all the way to a wide bend: this is the medieval weir. Occasionally prone to flooding, the weir section of the path may require a small diversion from the riverbank to avoid the puddles.

Continue over a small wooden bridge to follow the river's edge for a further 300 m where the path crosses a short boardwalk before re-joining a wide track. Turn right along the wide track as it moves away from the river and re-enters the open area crossed at the start of the walk. Continue straight ahead until you see the bridge. Turn right and follow the track over the bridge, retracing your steps to the car park.

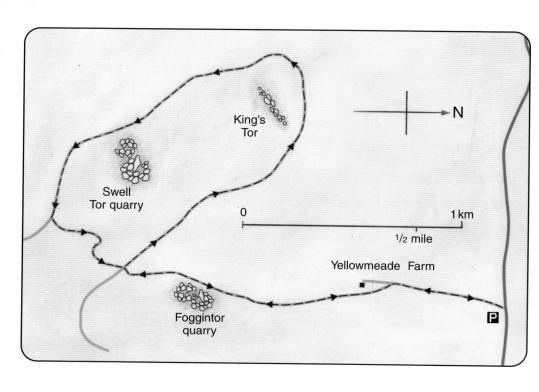

Walk 7 Kings Tor

Distance: 7 km   Pushchair type: All terrain
Character: Taking in two quarries and with wide-ranging views
towards Plymouth Sound on a clear day, this longer walk is on good
level tracks some of which used to form a railway line. The surface is
stony in places so the walk is only suitable for an all-terrain pushchair.

Park in the lay-by adjacent to the track for Yellowmeade Farm
(SX 567750). Follow this track heading out onto the moor; after 800 m
keep left, taking the track that runs above Yellowmeade Farm. After
passing the farm's field enclosures, you will soon reach Foggintor
Quarry where the ruins of the former quarry manager's cottage can
be seen and indeed some of the quarrymen's cottages too.

   Continue along the track for a further 450 m to a junction with
another track to the right. Take this right turn and shortly after turn
right again, joining the clearly defined track visible from a distance,
that contours around the hillside below King's Tor.

16

Follow the track around the Tor; on the north-western side you will find yourself overlooking the River Walkham Valley and on the opposite side Vixen Tor. Keep to the main track around the hillside, eventually passing below Swell Tor quarry. (If you are able to explore on foot, there are remains of carved stone corbels and the ruins of a blacksmith's shop to be seen.)

A short distance further on, take the track which rises to the left alongside a wall. Follow the track up the slope. It will soon return you to the main path junction just after Foggintor quarry; from here retrace your steps past Yellowmeade Farm back to your car.

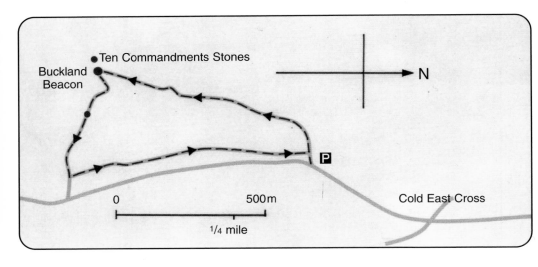

Walk 8 Buckland Beacon

Distance: 1.8 km or 2.3 km   Pushchair type: All terrain
Character: This short but scenic walk is on moorland which in a couple
of places is a little bumpy, but easily tackled by an all-terrain push-
chair. There are two options – an easy out and back route of 1.8 km, or
a circular route involving one or two stiles.

The destination is Buckland Beacon – a great place for a picnic, with
extensive views on a clear day. This lofty vantage point was and is used
as a fire beacon; local legend suggests it was where the Spanish Armada
was spotted from. It is also the location of the Ten Commandments
Stones, commissioned by the Lord of Buckland Manor in 1928.

Park in one of the laybys alongside the road (SX 739739) a few hun-
dred yards south-west of the Cold East Cross car park.

Leave the road, picking up the path that runs alongside the wall,
keeping the wall on your left-hand side. Follow this track along the
wall, keeping it on your left as it rounds a bend and climbs slightly.
Continue to follow this track up the ridge. There are a couple of
bumpy sections along this part of the track but plenty of space to skirt
round them to make the route easier on the pushchair. On reaching a
wall junction with a small stand of trees on the left, bear right up the
grassy track, heading towards the rocky outcrop on the skyline. Follow
this grassy track as it meanders towards the outcrop.

18

The outcrop you have reached is Buckland Beacon. If you walk round the tor to the left, you will discover the Ten Commandments Stones at the base of the outcrop. If you wish to take the easier version of this walk, return to your car by retracing your steps. Use the wall to guide you back, keeping it on your right hand side.

For the more adventurous, leave the Beacon heading in an easterly direction, walking towards the wall and the stile that crosses it. Carefully lift the pushchair over the wall (taking your little one out first) and use the stile to cross the wall. (For an easier crossing, follow the wall downhill for a short distance to a gate. Pass through the gate and walk back up the hill to the path leading away from the stile.)

Follow the grassy path, still heading in an easterly direction to reach a smaller second outcrop known as Welstor Rock.

The track continues eastwards. Follow it down the gentle slope, keeping right at a Y-junction until you reach the T-junction at the end of the path. Turn left here and follow the track as it meanders through the gorse and heather, eventually emerging onto a grassy section of ground. To the left you will notice an old stone building: this is the remains of the Welstor Rifle Range which was used by the Ashburton Rifle Volunteers between 1861 and 1900.

Head for the gap in the wall ahead of you and after passing through it, walk in a northerly direction to pick up an initially indistinct path. Aim towards the stand of trees on the skyline, which is where you parked your car. Just before reaching the road, you will encounter the second stile over the wall. Carefully negotiate it as the first one.

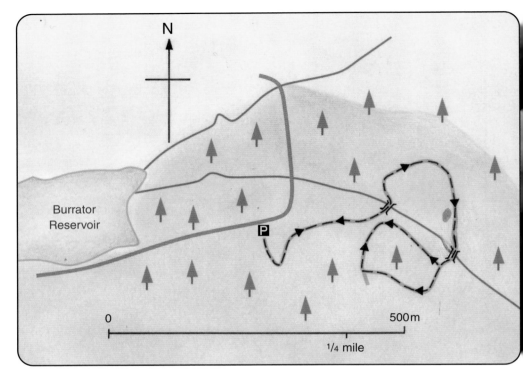

Walk 9 Burrator Arboretum

Distance: 1 km   Pushchair type: Any
Character: A super-easy stroll through the arboretum which was
planted after the storms of the late 1980s. There is a network of easy to
follow paths that criss-cross the site which you can explore at leisure,
but this circular route passes the main areas of interest with the chance
to spot some wildlife along the way.

Park in the Arboretum car park (SX 569690) and take the path through the gate into the woods. There are a number of little fauna and flora information boards along the way. Turn left at the first path junction and follow the path straight ahead. After approximately 40 m go left at the junction where you will shortly reach a wooden bridge over Narrator Brook. This is a great place to play Pooh-sticks!

Cross the bridge and continue straight on, following a bend in the path and up a slight slope. Continue past the large tree following the same path and after a further 100 m you will reach Dragonfly Pond

on the right. There is a small viewing platform to enable visitors to get closer to the wildlife.

Return to the path heading in the direction you were going where you will shortly reach a second bridge over the brook. Here you can choose to take the shorter option of following the boardwalk along this pretty stream; it will return you to the first bridge. Turn left here and retrace your steps to the car park.

Alternatively, pass the boardwalk on your right and continue to follow the path. After 40 m it turns to the right. Continue to follow it around the bend and for a further 150 m until you reach a T-junction. Turn right here and follow the track until it takes you back to the first bridge. Turn left to retrace your steps to the car park.

Optional extra: Burrator has a tarmac road that circumnavigates the reservoir and has various parking places. There are many walks that can be had along sections of the road or indeed the whole loop for those wishing to explore the area further and with a few hours to spare. There is also a Discovery Centre on the western side of the Reservoir which is worth a visit.

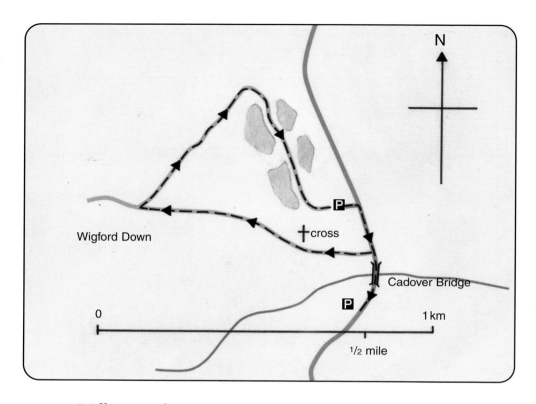

Walk 10 Cadover Bridge and Lakes

Distance: 2.8 km   Pushchair type: All terrain
Character: A short stroll across a lovely open section of the moor
passing an ancient cross and former China clay works which are now
rather beautiful angling lakes. The terrain is moorland track so is only
suitable for an all-terrain pushchair.

Park in the Cadover Bridge car park (SX 554645). Turn left out of the
car park, along the road and over the bridge. After a further 80 m, take
the dirt track on your left and follow it for 100 m until you see a path
on the right that heads up the slope.

Take this track which soon follows the line of a wall and opens
out into an indistinct green track passing Cadover Cross – one of a
number of crosses which mark the route that monks of the Priory at
Plympton used on their way to Tavistock Abbey. As the track reaches
the tip of the field enclosures, continue to walk straight ahead up the
slope where, after approximately 25 m, you will reach a path junction.

22

Turn right along this green track which runs along the hillside and starts to drop down towards the road.

After 50 m Cadover Lakes appear behind the spinney in the dip on your right hand side. Head towards the trees and carefully skirt the edge of the large depression, taking the path downhill between the two lakes. Follow this path across the track that runs from the road to the anglers' car park, passing a third lake on your left hand side.

Continue straight ahead to the largest of the lakes; the path follows the edge of the water before turning to the left and emerging in a large car park. Cross the car park and carefully re-join the road.

Turn right along the road and retrace your steps over Cadover Bridge to your car.

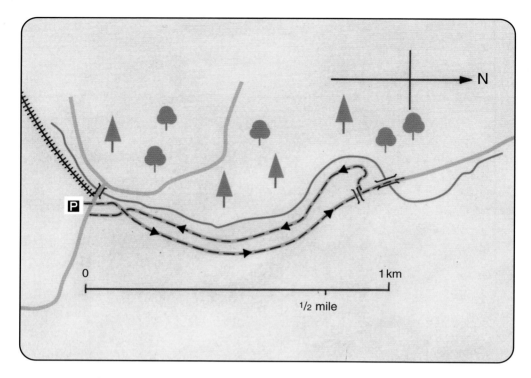

Walk 11 Plymbridge Woods

Distance: 2.5 km   Pushchair type: Options for all-terrain or any.
Character: An easy walk through a wooded valley, technically not on
Dartmoor but just outside, that was once a hive of industrial activity.
The route is along a former railway line and visits a viewing station
where peregrine falcons may be seen. There is a heritage railway service
that runs to Plymbridge station next to the car park so you may see a
steam train too.

Park in the National Trust car park at Plymbridge station (SX 524586).
Follow the signs NCR 27 up onto the former railway track at the end of
the station platform. Turn right; this is the National Cycle Route 27
which extends all the way to Tavistock.

Follow this track for 1 km where you will pass under a railway
bridge. Continue for another 20 m to the viaduct over the River Plym
where you will find the viewing platform and, if you are lucky, may
catch a glimpse of the peregrine falcons which nest on the cliff to the
right.

Option 1: If you are walking with a stroller or lightweight pushchair, this tarmac track continues for many kilometres. For a longer walk it can be followed to Bickleigh and then back to the car park by the same route covering a distance of 7.5 km in total.

For a shorter walk, from the peregrine platform retrace your steps along the track to the car park for a walk of 2 km in total.

Option 2: For those walking with an all-terrain or sturdy pushchair there is a circular route to follow. From the peregrine viewing station turn around and walk back to the bridge that you previously walked under.

Turn right, taking the gravel path up the slope. Follow the track straight ahead. It starts to drop downhill and round a bend towards the bank of the river. Follow this path as it runs between the old canal to the left and the river to the right. This track will take you all the way back to the start of the route where you will emerge from underneath a bridge opposite the car park entrance.

There-and-back walks

Walk 12   Meldon Viaduct

Distance: 7.5 km   Pushchair type: Any
Character: A potentially lengthy walk along a tarmac track, running
alongside the old Meldon railway line from Okehampton. Starting from
the restored Okehampton Station car park (also the location of a café,
museum and YHA hostel) the route follows the Granite Way cycle track
up onto the edge of the moor. Views from the viaduct at the end of
the walk take in Meldon Reservoir dam and the fascinating industrial
ruins of a quarry and mine.

Park in Okehampton Station car park (SX 587940). This station has
been recently re-commissioned after 50 years and is now a destination
for trains from Exeter.

   Leave the car park heading right down the road underneath the
railway bridge. Carefully cross the road and take the first left, signposted THE GRANITE WAY. Follow the road for approximately 100 m
then turn left onto the cycle path, following the Granite Way signs.
After 600 m if you look out over the trees to the right, there is a view
of the remains of the 11th century Okehampton Castle.

   Continue to follow the cycle track as it runs alongside the currently
unused train line to Meldon Viaduct. After a further 1300 m the track
reaches a gate and goes underneath the A30 emerging at a path junction. Take the metal gate next to the wooden gate – still following the
cycle route signs. The route follows the edge of Meldon woods for
1.5 km before arriving at Meldon Viaduct station. Walk past the station
for views from the viaduct towards the moor and of the remnants of
the limestone mine below. Return to your car by retracing your steps.

Walk 13   Golden Dagger Mine

Distance: 3 km   Pushchair type: All-terrain
Character: An easy route for an all-terrain pushchair, which can get
muddy in wet weather; note that there is a bit of a hill on the return
route. The walk visits the remains of two tin mines – Golden Dagger
and Vitifer – that were still in use in the 1930s. There is evidence that
this area was mined as far back as the Bronze Age.

Park in the small car park (SX676811) on the south-eastern side of the road within sight of the Warren House Inn. Take the distinct track eastwards from the car park, heading away from the main road. Continue to follow it for approximately 500 m ignoring tracks branching off to the side. The track starts to gently descend the hill and soon bends to the left before coming back on itself to deposit you amongst the Vitifer Mine workings. At the bottom of the hill you will soon reach a lovely spot with a grassy area and stream which makes a good stopping point for a picnic. (Beware of hidden mine-workings if exploring off the track.)

Continue straight ahead along the track, now heading southwards towards the forest ahead, known as Soussons Plantation. On reaching a gate, go straight through; shortly you will reach a signpost. Turn right here towards some ruined buildings: these are the first remains you will see of the Golden Dagger Mine. Retrace your steps to the signpost and continue to follow the track southwards to the next ruin where there is an information board. Once you have explored these ruins, retrace your steps to return to your car.

Walk 14 Princetown to Nun's Cross

Distance: 8 km   Pushchair type: Any
Character: A purpose built accessible track forming an easy out-and-
back route onto a remote part of the moor. Whilst the track is well
surfaced it would be easiest for an all-terrain or rugged pushchair
although not impossible with a stroller.

Park in the visitors' car park in the centre of Princetown next to the
High Moorland Visitor Centre (SX 589735). Leave the car park, walking in front of the Visitor Centre towards the Plume of Feathers pub
at the road junction. Cross the road and turn down the tarmac lane
next to the pub. After 40 m join the track marked PUBLIC BRIDLEWAY
and shortly after, go through a gate. Continue along this path for
another 300 m to another gate, pass through this and follow the gravel

28

track out onto the moor. After approximately 1.2 km you will reach South Hessary Tor close to the footpath. For a shorter walk of 3 km in total, stop here before retracing your steps to along the same path to Princetown. For the longer walk, continue to follow the track all the way to Nun's Cross, the furthest point of the walk, before retracing your steps back to your car.

Walk 15   The Swincombe Valley and Fairy Bridge

Distance: 2 km   Pushchair type: Any
Character: This short out-and-back walk is on excellent track including tarmac road surface so is accessible to all pushchairs. There are a couple of steep sections but you are rewarded with the perfect picnic spot at the Fairy Bridge and an opportunity to paddle in the River Swincombe. This area used to be a bustling centre of activity as it was the site of Gobbet Tin Mine whose ruins you will pass through. Just across the Fairy Bridge are the ruins of John Bishop's house which can be explored on foot leaving the pushchair by the bridge.

The starting point for this walk is alongside the lane leading to Sherberton which is a no through road. There is a small parking area on the right hand side (SX 651728), just before a gate and cattle grid marked SHERBERTON FARM.

Leave the car and walk through the gate marked SHERBERTON FARM, heading downhill on the lane for approximately 300 m. At the bottom of the hill, take the track that bears left through another gate, taking you past the remains of the Gobbet Tin Mine. Continue to follow this track as it meanders alongside the mine workings. After approximately 700 m the track rounds a bend and you will see the Fairy Bridge, the destination of this walk, slightly further ahead on the right hand side.

On reaching the bridge you will notice all three traditional methods here of crossing a river – stepping stones, a bridge and a ford. The ruins that are situated just across the bridge are fun to explore but are often waterlogged and muddy. If you want to venture across you will need to leave the pushchair near the bridge.

Return to the track and turning left retrace your steps back to the car.

The Fairy Bridge (Walk 15)

Walk 16 Holne

Distance: 3.5 km   Pushchair type: All terrain
Character: This stroll from Holne takes you through the fields down to the edge of the beautiful River Dart. It is downhill on the outward route and uphill on the way back; the rougher nature of the path in places means it is really only suitable for an all-terrain pushchair.

Park in the Holne village hall car park (SX 706695) – note the sign to users at the entrance. Turn right out of the car park and head along the road passing the 13th century church on your left. At the road junction turn right then immediately left, ASHBURTON PRINCETOWN. Continue straight ahead to the next junction (BUTTS CROSS); turn left here looking out for a wooden finger-post on the right, FOOTPATH NEWBRIDGE, also initialled MW for Mariners Way, an ancient coast-to-coast route.

Follow this path by the hedgerow until it emerges at the corner of a field. The path takes you diagonally across this and two other fields before joining the wood approximately 350 m further down the hill. On a clear day there are great views of the moor opposite.

Continue to follow the path into Holne Woods as it descends to the river. On reaching the riverbank you will see Horseshoe Falls and Salters Pool. Continue to follow the path along the river until it emerges onto the road next to Holne New Bridge. With care, cross the road to reach the car park and adjacent grassy area with toilet facilities and a refreshment van. This is the furthest point of the walk. To return to your car, retrace your steps over the bridge and take the path back through the woods.

Optional extra: Spitchwick is a fantastic river-swimming spot and place for a picnic a little further upstream. However, it is not easy to reach with a pushchair. For those feeling strong/able to carry the pushchair or with older children, take the path from the corner of New Bridge car park near the road and follow it under the bridge. After a short distance, the path goes up a steep incline with many tree roots to negotiate before opening into an easier path on the other side of the hill. Continue to follow this path to reach a wide and open grassy area next to a deep section of river; this is Spitchwick.

Walk 17 Avon Dam

Distance: 5.9 km   Pushchair type: Any
Character: This is an easy stroll along a tarmac road alongside the beautiful River Avon. The road emerges onto moorland giving you the experience of being on the moor whilst enjoying a firm surface underfoot.

Park in the Shipley Bridge car park (SX 681629); you will find a toilet block and signboard with interesting information about the area.

Take the footpath that runs next to the toilet block which shortly joins the metalled road – this road is only used by South West Water and contractors, so traffic is infrequent. Turn left onto the road following it upstream. After 300 m note the Hunter's Stone at the road junction in memory of local huntsmen who died in the World Wars.

Continue straight ahead on the main road where after a further 200 m you will pass the ruins of Brent Moor House. Continue to follow the road up the valley; now on open moorland, you will soon see your first glimpses of the dam on the horizon. After a sweeping bend to the left there is a track ascending a hill to the right. Here you have a choice.

Option 1: If you are using a stroller or prefer easier terrain, continue along the tarmac road which will take you to the foot of the dam.

Option 2: If you are using an all-terrain or sturdy pushchair, take the path to the right, following it all the way up the slope to the corner of the dam for views of the water. Retrace your steps to your car.